Welcome!!!

First, I want to say 'Congratulations' on continuing your journey to financial freedom. It won't be easy, but I guarantee it will be worth it.

Some of these financial concepts may take time to understand, some you may already know; either way feel free to discuss them with an adult.

This workbook is going to provide you with the knowledge and skills to be 'financially lit ' It's up to you to be DISCIPLINED to achieve your financial goals.

Best regards,

The Financial Literacy Guy

Assets vs Liabilities

The name of the game is to have your assets pay for your liabilities! We all know that an asset appreciates in value. It is best practice to let the appreciation of your asset offset a liability.

For every liability, you should have an asset that covers that expense. For example, you can have a rental property pay for your permanent residence, or you can have a car on Turo pay for your dream car.

	Asset	Liability
1. A car used for Uber Eats, Lyft, Turo, etc.	☐	☐
2. You	☐	☐
3. A House You Live In	☐	☐
4. A Rental Property	☐	☐
5. A Mercedes Benz	☐	☐
6. A Rolex	☐	☐
7. A Trademark	☐	☐
8. Jordan 1's	☐	☐
9. A Stock Portfolio	☐	☐

Answer Key:

Assets- 1,2,3,4,6,7,8,9

Liabilities- 5,8

To break the cycle of living paycheck-to-paycheck, you need to have a plan for your money. You need to know what money is coming in, and what money is going out. **A budget is a plan for your money!**

INCOME 1	INCOME 2	OTHER INCOME	TOTAL INCOME
+	+	=	

FIXED EXPENSES	BUDGETED	ACTUAL

VARIABLE EXPENSES	BUDGETED	ACTUAL

DEBT/SAVINGS	BUDGETED	ACTUAL

	BUDGETED	ACTUAL
TOTAL INCOME		
FIXED EXPENSES −		
VARIABLE EXPENSES −		
DEBT/SAVINGS −		
TOTAL LEFTOVER =		

CREDIT CARD FAQS

CREDIT REPORTING AGENCIES

- **Transunion** 800-916-8800 transunion.com
- **Experian** 866-617-1894 experian.com
- **Equifax** 888-298-0045 equifax.com

REMINDER 1

FREE REPORT

You're entitled to one free credit report a year

*Make sure everything being reported is accurate.

*www.annualcreditreport.com

THINGS TO CONSIDER WHEN CHOOSING A CREDIT CARD

- **$0 Annual Fee (avoid credit cards with annual fees, unless the benefits are worth it)**
- **Rewards and Benefits (cash back, airline miles, etc.)**
- **Take advantage of 0% Interest Introductory Period**
- **Purchase APR Interest Rate**

CREDIT HACK

15/3 Payment

A credit optimization strategy where you make two credit card payments in one month. You make one payment 15 days before your statement date and then the second payment, 3 days before that same statement date.

GOOD RULES & HABITS TO PRACTICE

Discipline

Stay within your **budget**. Do not overspend or abuse your credit. Only spend what you can pay back.

PAY IN FULL

Do Not carry a balance! You should be only spending what you can **pay back in full** and on time.

DEBIT CARD

A debit card is a payment card that deducts money directly from a consumer's checking account when it is used. Also called "check cards" or "bank cards."

Although Debit Cards, ATM Cards, and Credit cards all look similar; they're different.

Debit Card (your money)- Swiping a debit card is exactly like writing a check. Specifically, debit cards are associated with the bank where you have your checking account. When you make a purchase with your debit card, the purchase price is deducted from your checking account balance.

ATM Card (your money)- Similar to a debit card, the money is deducted from your bank account. However, this card can only be used at the ATM for cash withdrawals (it does not have a Visa, Mastercard, or Discover card logo to be used for purchases).

Credit Card (not your money)- A credit card is issued to consumers to make purchases, with the agreement that the cardholder will pay back the card issuer the cost of the item, along with any agreed upon fees and interest. Essentially, a credit card acts as a loan that allows you to make purchases now and pay it off within 30 days. If you pay after 30 days you may pay more because of interest.

DIRECT DEPOSIT

Direct Deposit is the deposit of funds electronically into a bank account, rather than receiving a physical, paper check. It is a fast, safe, convenient way to receive payment. In order to receive funds you must provide your employer with your bank information (account & routing number). Because the funds are electronically transferred, you do not have to wait for the money to clear. The money is automatically on your debit card.

en·tre·pre·neur

en·tre·pre·neur
noun
the crazy people who work 100 hours a week for themselves so they don't have to work 40 hours for someone else.

a person who risks their own money for freedom, rather than exchanging their freedom for money

Entrepreneurship isn't for everyone. But I encourage everyone to see if it is for them.

There are several types of Entrepreneurs and several types of entrepreneurship styles, yet they all possess similar characteristics.

Types of Entrepreneurs:

- Builder
- Opportunist
- Innovator
- Specialist

Types of Entrepreneurship:

- Small Business Entrepreneurship
- Scalable Startup
- Large Company
- Social Entrepreneurship

Personality Characteristics:

- Versatile
- Flexible
- Money Savvy
- Resilient
- Focused
- Business Smart
- Communicators

FICA

Federal Insurance Contribution Act

Not to be confused with FICO (FICO deals with your credit score)

When you get paid, taxes will be taken out of your check. One of the taxes taken out is FICA.

FICA is a U.S. Payroll Tax. FICA helps fund both Social Security and Medicare programs. Both programs provide benefits for retirees, the disabled, and children.

-6.2% of your gross wages goes to Social Security Taxes
-1.45% of your gross wages goes to Medicare

**Your employer matches these percentages for a total of 15.3%*

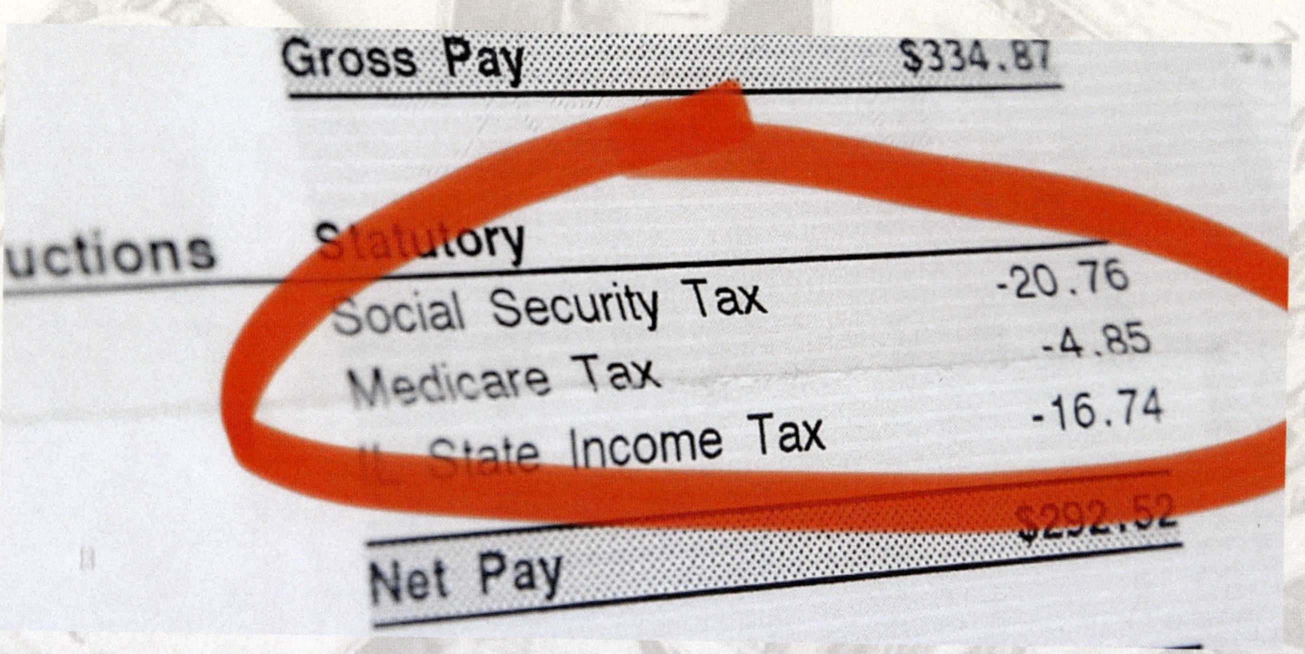

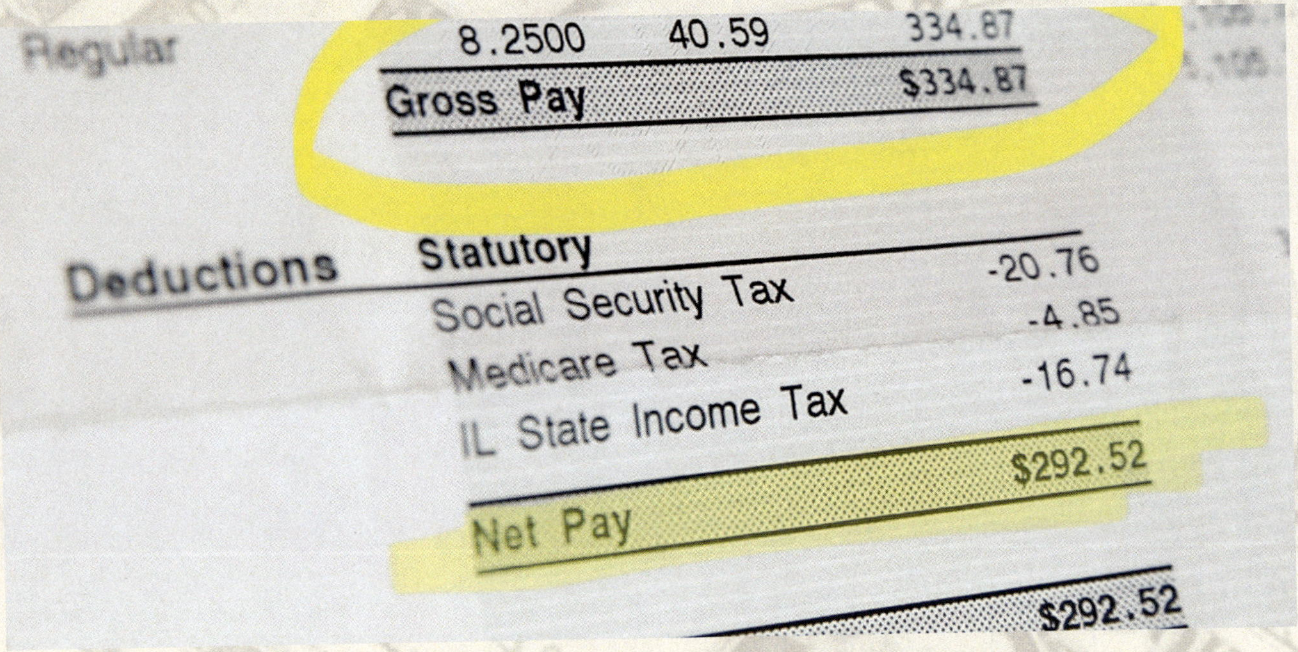

Gross Income is your income **before taxes**. It is your total pay **before** any taxes or other deductions are taken out. Gross annual income is the amount of money that a person earns in one year **before taxes**, and includes income from all sources.

To calculate your gross income multiply your hourly rate times the hours worked.

In the example above we can see the gross income is the hourly rate of $8.50 multiplied by the 40.59 hours worked; giving a gross income of $334.87.

One of the benefits of owning a home is building equity in your property.

Home Equity is the value of a homeowners stake in their property, as opposed to the lenders stake.

To calculate your **home equity**; you divide the amount you owe by the value of your home.

For example, say you owe $250,000 on a home worth $500,000. That's $250,000 / $500,000 = .50 or 50% loan to value (LTV). This means that you have 50% equity in your home. You own 50% outright.

How much equity do you have if you owe $100,000 and your house is worth $400,000?

a. 25%. b. 30%. c. 40%. d. 10%

Now here's where finance gets a little tricky. In finance, a single word may have multiple meanings; **interest** is one of those words. You have good interest (*APY*) and you have *bad* interest (*APR*).

APR vs APY

Good **interest (APY)** is the interest earned. APY is usually associated with deposit accounts. The higher the APY, the more return you're getting on your investment.

Bad **interest (APR)** is the interest charged. APR is associated with credit accounts. The lower the APR on your account, the lower the overall cost of borrowing might be.

JOB *versus* CAREER

Choose whether each example is a Job or a Career. Put a check mark ✔ in the box that represents the best answer.

	Job	Career
1. Something you only do for money	☐	☐
2. Full of networking opportunities	☐	☐
3. A series of connected employment opportunities	☐	☐
4. Has minimal impact on your future work life	☐	☐
5. Provides experience & learning to fuel your future	☐	☐
6. Offers few networking opportunities	☐	☐
7. Progressing towards lifelong goals	☐	☐
8. A journey that lasts your whole life	☐	☐
9. A long term endeavor	☐	☐

Answer Key:

Job - 1,4,6

Career - 2,3,5,7,8,9

Know
Your
Customer

KYC is an acronym for 'Know Your Customer'

A KYC Check is the mandatory standard of identifying and verifying clients identity when opening an account.

In other words, banks must make sure that their clients are genuinely who they claim to be.

Know Your Customer (KYC) is designed to protect financial institutions against fraud, corruption, money laundering, and terrorist financing.

**At times, you may need to confirm identity with a government/state issued photo ID, Social Security number, or proof of address documentation.*

There are many types of loans.

Some loans are good and can help you achieve your financial goals. While other loans use unfair or deceptive tactics; to entice a borrower into taking a **loan** that benefits the lender at the borrower's expense. These type of lenders are considered *predatory lenders*. Stay away from predatory lenders that appear as payday loans, ultra high interest rate loans, etc.

Some of the more common loans that will help you achieve your financial goals are **home loans**, **auto loans**, and **education loans**.

When choosing a loan, a few things you should consider are APR, term of loan, loan options, monthly payments, etc.

Money Quiz

There are no right or wrong answers; simply respond as you see fit and see what you discover about yourself.

- Score 2 points for each 'Yes', 1 point for each 'S / Sometimes', and 0 points for 'No'.

		Yes	S	No
1.	I have good saving habits	☐	☐	☐
2.	I have SMART financial goals	☐	☐	☐
3.	My money works hard for me	☐	☐	☐
4.	I have an emergency savings	☐	☐	☐
5.	I invest my money	☐	☐	☐
6.	I say "No" to others when I need to	☐	☐	☐
7.	I understand 'My Wants' versus 'My Needs'	☐	☐	☐
8.	My current budget is up-to-date	☐	☐	☐
9.	I have things to look forward to in my life	☐	☐	☐

Your total score ______ **/18**

Net Income = Gross Income - Total Deductions

Hours and Earnings			Taxes and Deductions	
Hours	**Rate**	**Earnings**	**Description**	**Amount**
80	$27.00	$2160.00	Federal Tax	$296.75
			State Tax	$97.38
			Social Security	$81.41
			Medicare	$28.1[illegible]

Gross Year-to-Date	Gross This Pay Period	Total Deductions	Net Pay
$8640.00	$2160.00	$503.64	$1656.36

Let's take a look at this sample paycheck.

Here, you worked 80 hours at a rate of $27 per hour.

How much did you gross for this pay period? ______________

If you answered $2,160 you are correct.

Sad to say, you don't take home $2,160. You have to factor in all your deductions; FICA and any additional taxes or expenses.

What are your total deductions for this pay period? ______________

If you said your total deductions were $503.64, you are correct.

Now, that we know how much you grossed and your total deductions, let's calculate your **Net Income**.

$2160.00 - $503.64 = $1656.36

Overdraft Protection is a 'funds transfer' option offered to bank accounts that protects a balance from going below zero.

The idea is that a savings account, or another account with the available funds, is protecting the primary checking account balance from going below zero and incurring any overdraft fees or non-sufficient fees (NSF).

How It Works:

A person is writing a $1000 deposit check for an office space they're going to lease. Here's how that situation would play out **with and without overdraft protection.**

With Overdraft Protection		Without Overdraft Protection	
Total Deposit to Pay	$1000	Total Deposit to Pay	$1000
Payment from Checking	-$700	Payment from Checking	-$1000
Overdraft Amount	$300	CHECK BOUNCES	
Overdraft Fee	$35	NSF Fee	$30
Total Left to Pay	**$335**	**Total Left to Pay**	**$1030**

**Try to avoid using a credit card as the Overdraft Protecting account. The transfer of funds is normally charged as a cash advance.*

PASSIVE *Income*

I heard someone say, "You're not making money, until you're making money while you sleep", that's what **Passive Income** is.

Below are several passive income ideas. Choose **Yes** or **No** to decide whether or not it is an idea you can see yourself doing.

	Yes	No
1. Create an app	☐	☐
2. Have a Rental Property	☐	☐
3. Own Dividend Stocks	☐	☐
4. Create a Blog or Youtube Channel	☐	☐
5. Rent Out Your Home Short Term	☐	☐
6. Advertise On Your Car	☐	☐
7. Flip Retail Products	☐	☐
8. Affiliate Marketing	☐	☐
9. REITs, Bonds, or High Yield Savings Account	☐	☐

Now that you've identified what passive income ideas you can see yourself doing, let's narrow them down and come up with a plan on how you're going to accomplish it.

QUALIFIED RETIREMENT ACCOUNT

QUALIFIED RETIREMENT ACCOUNTS INCLUDE:

- 401(K) Plans
- 403(B) Plans
- Profit Sharing Plans
- Keogh (HR-10) Plans

QUALIFIED VS NON- QUALIFIED

Qualified Plans

- Meet ERISA guidelines
- Qualify for certain tax benefits and government protections.

Non-Qualified Plans

- Do Not meet all ERISA stipulations
- Deducted contributions are taxed when income is recognized

QUALIFIED PLANS EITHER HAVE

- **Defined-Contribution-** Employees select investments and retirement account is determined by investments.
- **Defined-Benefit-** There is a guaranteed payout amount

**IRA's are NOT created by an employer, so therefore are not qualified plans*

IN LAYMAN TERMS:

Qualified plans have <u>tax-deferred</u> contributions from the employee, and employers may deduct amounts they contribute to the plan.

Non-Qualified plans use after-tax dollars to fund them, and in most cases employers cannot claim their contributions as a tax deduction.

Return On Investment (ROI) is a ratio that compares the gain or loss of an investment compared to its cost. Even though it is a ratio it is expressed as a percentage.

$$\text{ROI} = \frac{\text{Net Return on Investment}}{\text{Cost of Investment}} \times 100\%$$

Second method:

$$\text{ROI} = \frac{\text{FVI} - \text{IVI}}{\text{Cost of Investment}} \times 100\%$$

where:

$\text{FVI} = \text{Final value of investment}$

$\text{IVI} = \text{Initial value of investment}$

For Example:

Assume you purchase 1,000 shares of a company at $10 per share. One year later, you sell the shares for $12.50. You also earned dividends of $500 over the one-year holding period. You also spent a total of $125 on trading commissions in order to buy and sell the shares.

$$\text{ROI} = \frac{(\$12.50 - \$10) \times 1000 + \$500 - \$125}{\$10 \times 1000} \times 100$$

$$= 28.75\%$$

"First you save your money, then your money saves you."

Saving is at the foundation of being financially lit.

You have to be able to budget in order to save. After you save, you're able to invest and have your money work hard for you, instead of you working hard for money.

Saving won't get you rich. These are not the times when your grandparents used to get 10% on their savings accounts. You're more likely to get .10% on a savings account. However, being able to save allows for two things: NOT living paycheck-to-paycheck and being ready in case of an emergency.

There are different types of savings accounts offered by financial institutions. You have your standard savings account that normally serves as Overdraft Protection for your checking account, as well as other savings accounts offered by financial institutions such as money market accounts and CD's.

Money market accounts and CD's offer slightly higher interest rates on your money.

Taxes

There are two types of taxation: Direct Taxes and Indirect Taxes.

Direct taxes are taxes taken directly from an individual or businesses wealth.

Indirect taxes are taxes only taken when an expenditure is made.

Types of Taxes

- Sales Tax
- Sin Tax
- Travel Tax
- Value-Added Tax
- Property Tax
- Capital Gains Tax
- Inheritance/Estate Tax
- Payroll Tax
- Income Tax

** Tax revenues finance government activities; including public works and services such as roads and schools, or programs such as Social Security and Medicare*

Uniform Transfers to Minors Act (UTMA) accounts are custodial accounts, held in the name of the minor, but controlled by a parent or guardian until the child reaches the age of 18.

This type of account allows you to transfer financial assets to a minor without establishing a trust.

The **Uniform Transfer to Minors Act (UTMA**) also allows minors to own other types of property, such as real estate, fine art, patents and royalties, and for the transfers to occur through inheritance.

Similarly, The *Uniform Gift to Minors Act (UGMA)* established a simple way for a minor to own securities without requiring trust documents or the court appointment of a trustee.

Anything that does not have a set value is a **variable**.

Most **variable** rate consumer loans are tied to one of two benchmark rates, the London Interbank Offered Rate, known as LIBOR, or the Prime Rate.

In finance, stock prices, earnings, dividend payments, interest rates, and gross domestic product (GDP) are all examples of variables.

In general, **variable** rate loans tend to have lower interest rates than fixed, because they are more riskier.

For consumers who can afford to take risks, or plan to pay their loan off quickly, **variable** rate loans are a good option.

Before committing to a loan it is best to consider your personal financial situation. Considering these factors can help dictate whether you should choose a fixed rate or variable rate loan.

It's one thing to be 'rich', it's another thing to be wealthy.

Wealth measures the value of all assets owned by a person, business, organization, or nation. Essentially, wealth is the accumulation of scarce resources or goods; gold, land, oil, etc.

Wealth consists of many aspects; like our health, relationships, finances, and time; and can be broken down into four categories:

Money (Financial Wealth)
Status (Social Wealth)
Freedom (Time Wealth)
Health (Physical Wealth)

Wealthy people spend less than they earn and invest their money to build long-term, sustainable wealth; generational wealth.

Generational Wealth is wealth that gets transferred from one generation to another.

XD refers to a stock trading Ex-Dividend. Sometimes 'X' alone is used to indicate a stock is trading ex-dividend.

A stock trading Ex-Dividend is a stock that trades without the value of the next dividend payment.

If you purchase a stock after it has gone Ex-Dividend, you will own the stock but will not get the next dividend payment for that stock. Instead the dividend payment will go to the person who sold you the stock.

*Stocks trading immediately past the dividend distribution may be lower in price, by the amount of the cash dividend payout.

Yield = Net Realized Return / Principal Amount

Yields measure the realized return on a security over a set period of time. It can also vary based on the invested security, the duration of investment, and the return amount.

Yield on Stocks

For stock-based investments, two types of yields are popularly used: cost yield and current yield. When calculated based on the purchase price, the yield is called yield on cost (YOC), or cost yield, and is calculated as:

Cost Yield = (Price Increase + Dividends Paid) / Purchase Price

However, many investors may like to calculate the yield based on the current market price, instead of the purchase price. This yield is referred to as the current yield and is calculated as:

Current Yield = (Price Increase + Dividend Paid) / Current Price

Yield to Maturity

YTM is the average yield expected per year and the value is expected to remain constant throughout the holding period until the maturity of the bond.

Yield to Call

YTC refers to the bond's yield at the time of its call date on *callable bonds*

Yield on Bonds

The yield on bonds that pay annual interest can be calculated in a straightforward manner—called the nominal yield, which is calculated as:

Nominal Yield = (Annual Interest Earned / Face Value of Bond)

**However, the yield on a floating interest rate bond will vary because the interest paid is variable.*

"**Zero-Percent**" promotional interest rate offers can be your best friend or your worst enemy; it's up to you.

Although **zero-percent** financing might seem beneficial, consumers should be aware of hidden fees and should ensure that they are able to fully repay the debt once the promotional period has expired.

Zero Percent offers typically last for only a limited period of time; six months or one year. After the promotional period has ended, any unpaid balance will typically be charged at a much higher interest rate. If the consumer has not paid off the debt in full, they might find themselves surprised by the sudden increase in monthly payments.

Ultimately, stores that offer **zero-percent** financing are hoping that many consumers fail to pay off the full balance of their purchase by the time the promotional period is over. They hope to benefit from the much higher interest rates charged afterward. Don't let them!!!

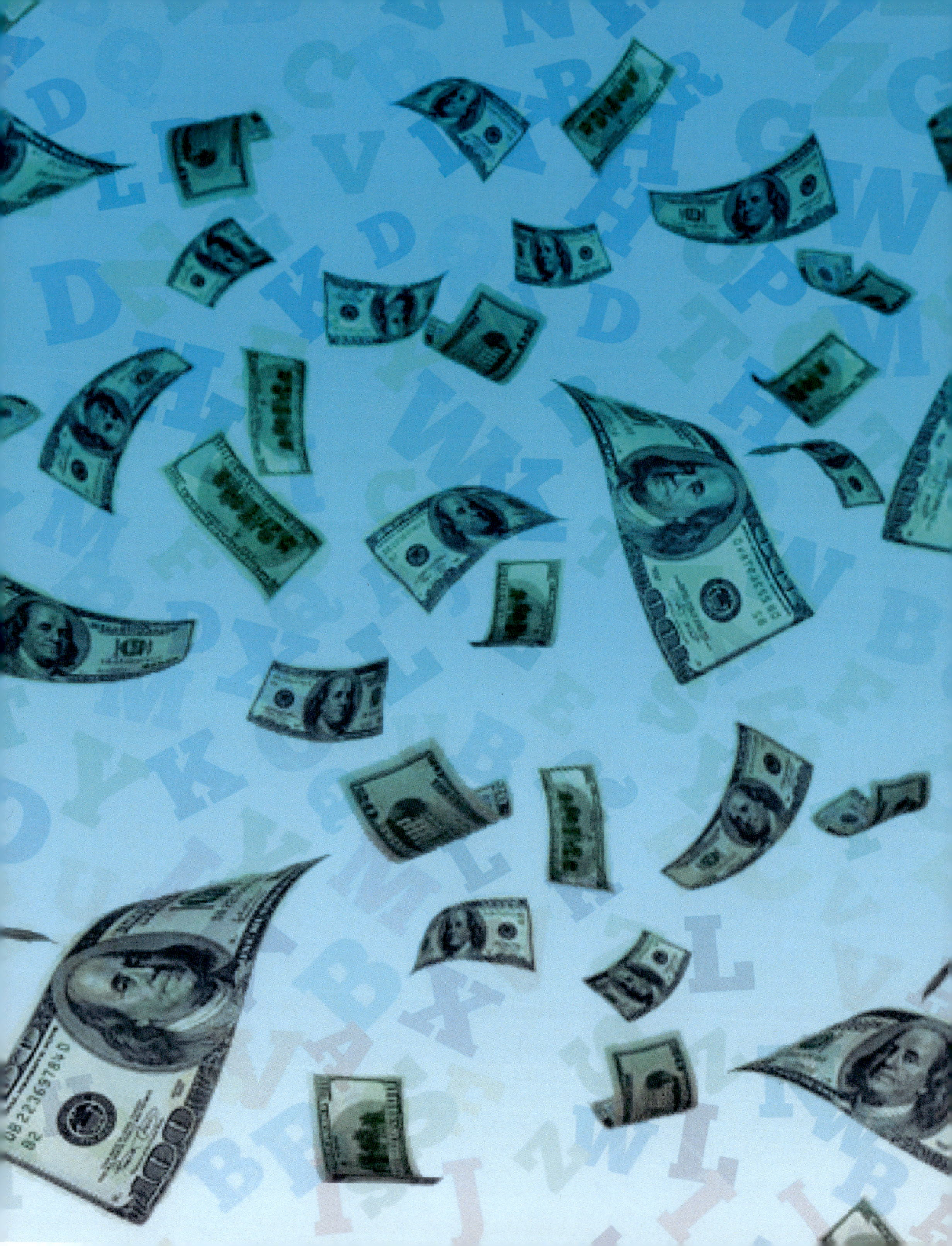